How To Study:

EASY **I AM YOUR GRAMMAR**

Work Book **2**

I**am** books

Contents

B

Chapter 1
Nouns and Pronouns

unit 1 Plural Nouns

Grammar focus

1. 명사에 -ves를 왜 붙이나요?

명사 끝이 -f(e)로 끝나는 명사는 -f(e)를 지우고 -ves를 붙여서 복수형을 만들어요.

2. 어떤 명사에 -ies를 붙이나요?

명사 끝이 〈자음+y〉로 끝나는 명사는 -y를 i로 고치고 -es를 붙여요.

하지만, ay, -ey, -oy로 끝나는 단어는 그냥 -s만 붙여요. -ies를 붙이지 않아요.

ex) boy – boy**s**   monkey – monkey**s**   day – day**s**

-f(e) ➡ -ves		-y ➡ -ies	
a leaf	➡ leaves	a baby	➡ babies
a wolf	➡ wolves	a city	➡ cities
a knife	➡ knives	a lady	➡ ladies
a wife	➡ wives	a story	➡ stories
		a country	➡ countries
		a dictionary	➡ dictionaries

Usage

~ves

There is a lea**f**.   There are lea**ves**.

I have a kni**fe**.   I have kni**ves**.

~ies

There is a pup**py**.   There are pup**pies**.

I see a ba**by**.   I see two ba**bies**.

6

Go for it!

A. Look and circle the correct word.

1.

three (leavs / (leaves))

2.

two (wolfs / wolves)

3.

two (wifes / wives)

4.

three (candys / candies)

B. Choose and write.

city   leaf   baby   wolf   lady   knife   candy   story   country   wife

- ies

- ves

1. _____cities_____   2. _____

3. _____   4. _____

5. _____   6. _____

7. _____   8. _____

9. _____   10. _____

C. Fill in the blanks and rewrite the sentences.

1. It ____is____ a knife. ➡ *They are knives* .

2. It _____ an apple. ➡ _____ .

3. She _____ a lady. ➡ _____ .

4. It is _____ orange. ➡ _____ .

5. It is _____ box. ➡ _____ .

6. It _____ a city. ➡ _____ .

7. It _____ a dictionary. ➡ _____ .

D. Circle the correct word and write.

1.
   dictionary
   (dictionaries)
   I have two ____*dictionaries*____ .

2. wolfves
   wolves
   We see four _____ .

3. countrys
   countries
   There are many _____ .

4. puppves
   puppies
   I have three _____ .

Grammar in Writing

A. Look and write answers.

1.

   Q: Do you want a puppy? (three)
   A: *No, I don't* . *I want 3(three) puppies* .

2. Q: Do you want an orange? (two)
   A: _____ . _____ .

3. Q: Do you see a lady? (two)
   A: _____ . _____ .

4. Q: Does she have a knife? (five)
   A: _____ . _____ .

B. Rewrite the sentences.

1. A leaf is on the table. → (4) *Four leaves are on the table* .

2. A baby is in the room. → (5) _____ .

3. A dictionary is on the desk. → (2) _____ .

4. They have a puppy. → (3) _____ .

5. There is a thief. → (2) _____ .

6. There is a candy. → (6) _____ .

unit 2 Irregular Plural Nouns

Grammar focus

a woman

two **women**

1. 불규칙이 뭐예요?

보통 명사에 -s나 -es를 붙이는 것을 규칙변화라고 하고, 불규칙은 일정한 규칙이 없이 자체의 복수형을 갖는 것을 말해요.

Irregular Plural Nouns(불규칙 복수명사)			
a man	➡ men	a woman	➡ women
a tooth	➡ teeth	a foot	➡ feet
a mouse	➡ mice	a fish	➡ fish
a deer	➡ deer	a goose	➡ geese
a sheep	➡ sheep	a child	➡ children

Usage

a child ➡ **children**

a deer ➡ **deer**

a mouse ➡ **mice**

a foot ➡ **feet**

a woman ➡ **women**

a man ➡ **men**

Go for it!

A. Write the plural form of each word.

1. a woman ➡ *women*

2. a man ➡ _____

3. a mouse ➡ _____

4. a foot ➡ _____

5. a tooth ➡ _____

6. a goose ➡ _____

7. a fish ➡ _____

8. a sheep ➡ _____

9. a deer ➡ _____

10. a child ➡ _____

B. Count and write.

1.

I see _*three*_ _*puppies*_ .

2.

I see _____ _____ .

3.

I see _____ _____ .

4.

I see _____ _____ .

5.

I see _____ _____ .

6.

I see _____ _____ .

C. Change the sentences into singular forms.

1. These are fish. → *This is a fish* .

2. Those are mice. → _____ .

3. These are teeth. → _____ .

4. Those are deer. → _____ .

5. These are feet. → _____ .

6. Those are geese. → _____ .

7. These are sheep. → _____ .

D. Correct the mistakes.

1. There are five fishs.
   → *There are five fish* .

2. There are four woman.
   → _____ .

3. There are four foot.
   → _____ .

4. There are two child.
   → _____ .

5. There are three sheeps.
   → _____ .

Grammar in Writing

A. Read and write answers.

1.
   Q: Do you want a mouse?
   A: *No, I don't* . *I want two mice* .

2.
   Q: Does she have a goose?
   A: _____ . _____ .

3.
   Q: Does he have a fish?
   A: _____ . _____ .

4.
   Q: Do you see ten deer?
   A: _____ . _____ .

5.
   Q: Does he want a sheep?
   A: _____ . _____ .

6.
   Q: Do you see a woman?
   A: _____ . _____ .

unit 3 Coutable & Uncountable Noun

Grammar focus

Q: What's on the table?
A: Two apples, **bread**, and **milk**.

1. 셀 수 없는 명사가 뭐예요?

하나, 둘 (한 개, 두 개), 이렇게 수를 셀 수 없는 명사를 말해요.

2. 셀 수 없는 명사에는 -(e)s를 못 붙이나요?

네, 맞아요. 셀 수 없기 때문에 복수의 형태가 없이 단수형만 있으며, 관사 a(an)를 붙일 수 없어요.

Countable Nouns (셀 수 있는 명사)				Uncountable Nouns (셀 수 없는 명사)	
a bus	➡ buses	a cat	➡ cats	water	milk
a leaf	➡ leaves	a baby	➡ babies	paper	cheese
a watch	➡ watches	a boy	➡ boys	butter	bread
a lady	➡ ladies	a box	➡ boxes	rain	snow
a dish	➡ dishes	a fox	➡ foxes	coffee	tea
a city	➡ cities	a car	➡ cars	rice	salt
a man	➡ men	a woman	➡ women	information	money
				wine	pizza

Go for it!

A. Write *C* for countable nouns and *U* for uncountable nouns.

1.

(U) milk

2.

( ) puppy

3.

( ) coffee

4.

( ) paper

5.

( ) leaf

6.

( ) rice

B. Check and write.

1.

☑ It is juice.
☐ They are juice.

It is juice _____ .

2.

☐ It is eggs.
☐ They are eggs.

_____ .

3.

☐ It is pizza.
☐ They are pizza.

_____ .

4.

☐ It is money.
☐ They are money.

_____ .

C. Match and correct the sentence.

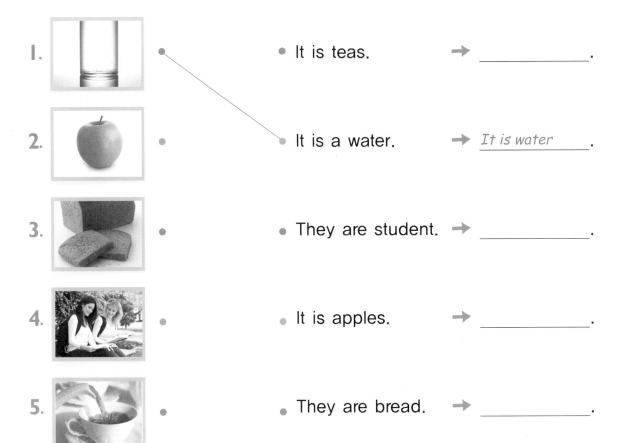

1. • ———————— • It is teas. → _____ .

2. • • It is a water. → *It is water* .

3. • • They are student. → _____ .

4. • • It is apples. → _____ .

5. • • They are bread. → _____ .

D. Write *a(an)* for countable nouns and X for uncountable nouns.

1. (*a*) lemon

2. (   ) butter

3. (   ) cheese

4. (   ) airplane

5. (   ) spaghetti

6. (   ) orange

Grammar in Writing

A. Look and write.

1.
(apple)
Q: What are they?
A: *They are apples* .

2.
(rice)
Q: What is it?
A: _____ .

3.
(leaf)
Q: What are they?
A: _____ .

4.
(orange juice)
Q: What is it?
A: _____ .

5.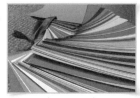
(paper)
Q: What is it?
A: _____ .

6.
(puppy)
Q: What are they?
A: _____ .

7.
(salt)
Q: What is it?
A: _____ .

8.
(pencil)
Q: What are they?
A: .

Grammar focus

There is **some** milk and there's a hamburger.

1. 부정관사가 뭐예요?

부정관사는 단수 명사 앞에서 한 명, 한 개, 하나를 나타내주는 a나 an을 가리켜 말하는 거예요.

2. some은 어떨 때 쓰는 건가요?

some은 우리말로 '약간의, 조금의'라는 뜻으로, 명사의 수와 양을 정확하게 모를 때 명사 앞에 사용하는 거예요. some은 셀 수 있는 명사, 셀 수 없는 명사 앞에 모두 쓸 수 있어요.

	Countable Noun	Uncountable Noun
a / an	a pencil an orange	juice coffee
some	some pencils some oranges	some juice some coffee

Usage

Countable Noun

He has **a** book.

She has **some** books.

Uncountable Noun

She has **some** milk.

I have **some** rice.

Go for it!

A. Circle the correct word.

1. (a / an / (some)) water
2. (a / an / some) orange juice

3. (a / an / some) cups
4. (a / an / some) salt

5. (a / an / some) elephant
6. (a / an / some) forks

7. (a / an / some) umbrella
8. (a / an / some) cheese

9. (a / an / some) butter
10. (a / an / some) knives

11. (a / an / some) bread
12. (a / an / some) book

13. (a / an / some) tiger
14. (a / an / some) children

15. (a / an / some) alligator
16. (a / an / some) spaghetti

17. (a / an / some) airplane
18. (a / an / some) paper

19. (a / an / some) puppies
20. (a / an / some) women

B. Write *a, an* or *some.*

1.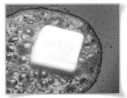

some butter

2.

_____ ant

3.

_____ leaves

4.

_____ money

5.

_____ flower

6.

_____ eggs

C. Complete the sentences.

1. We want some _____books_____. (book)

2. She drinks some _____. (tea)

3. I see some _____. (child)

4. They want some _____. (bread)

5. I have some _____ today. (homework)

6. He has some _____. (money)

7. I need some _____. (pencil)

Grammar in Writing

A. Complete the sentences with *some*.

1. I see _____some_____ _____women_____. (woman)

2. I have _____ _____. (puppy)

3. She has _____ _____. (money)

4. He has _____ _____. (milk)

5. We see _____ _____. (house)

6. I need _____ _____. (salt)

B. Look at the pictures and make sentences.

| money | bread | water | milk |

1.

(he / have)

He has some bread _____.

2.

(she / have)

_____.

3.

(The woman / have)

_____.

4.

(my mom / have)

_____.

unit 5 Mine / Yours / His / Hers ...

Grammar focus

Q: Is that **his** ball?
A: Yes, the ball is **his**.

1. 소유격 대명사가 뭐예요?

소유대명사도 대명사에요. 앞서 배웠던 my, your, her, his, their와 같은 소유격은 my book, your book, her book, his book처럼 반드시 뒤에 명사가 함께 붙어야 문장에서 역할을 할 수 있게 돼요. 이런 〈소유격+명사〉를 한 단어로 표현할 수 있는 대명사가 있는데 그것을 소유대명사라고 하는 거예요.

Subject Pronouns (주격)	Possessive Adj. (소유격)	Possessive Pronouns (소유 대명사)
I	my	mine (나의 것)
We	our	ours (우리의 것)
You	your	yours (너의 것)
He	his	his (그의 것)
She	her	hers (그녀의 것)
They	their	theirs (그들의 것)

Usage

Q: Is that **her** bicycle?
A: Yes, the bicycle is **hers**.

This is **my** cell phone.
The cell phone is **mine**.

Q: Is this **their** book?
A: Yes, the book is **theirs**.

A. Look and match.

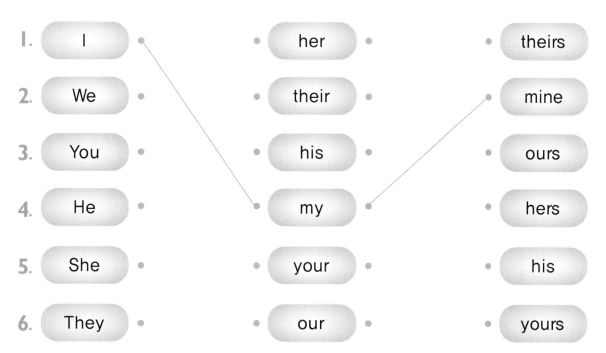

1. I	her	theirs
2. We	their	mine
3. You	his	ours
4. He	my	hers
5. She	your	his
6. They	our	yours

B. Circle the correct word.

1.

The books are (her / hers).

2.

The camera is (their / theirs).

3.

The glasses are (his / he).

4.

It is (yours / your) car.

C. Choose and write.

1.  This is ___my___ MP3 player. The MP3 player is ___mine___.
   (mine / my) (I / mine)

2.  That is _____ house. The house is _____.
   (they / their) (their / theirs)

3.  This is _____ pencil. The pencil is _____.
   (his / he) (his / he)

4.  That is _____ puppy. The puppy is _____.
   (she / her) (hers / her)

D. Fill in the blanks.

Subject Pronouns	Possessive Adjectives	Possessive Pronouns
_____	_____	mine
_____	our	_____
you	_____	_____
_____	his	_____
She	_____	_____
_____	their	_____

Grammar in Writing

A. Change the sentences.

1. This is my laptop. ➡ *The laptop is mine* _____.

2. That is your car. ➡ _____.

3. These are his sneakers. ➡ _____.

4. They are her flowers. ➡ _____.

5. This is our dictionary. ➡ _____.

6. That is their house. ➡ _____.

B. Read and make answers.

1. Q: Is this your book?
   A: No, *it isn't* _____. *It is his* _____. (he)

2. Q: Are these her glasses?
   A: No, _____. _____. (I)

3. Q: Is that his car?
   A: No, _____. _____. (she)

4. Q: Are these your skates?
   A: No, _____. _____. (they)

5. Q: Is this their bicycle?
   A: No, _____. _____. (we)

Chapter 2
Be-Verbs & Wh- questions

unit 1 *S+be* / *S+be+not*

Grammar focus

She **is** Tiffany.
They **are** teachers.
They **are** old.

He **is** Peter.
They **aren't** doctors.
They **aren't** young.

1. be동사가 뭐예요?

우리말로 '~이다'라는 의미로 주어와 be동사 뒤에 오는 말을 연결해 주는 역할을 해요.

2. be동사는 왜 모양이 다른가요?

우리말은 모두 '~이다'라고 하지만 영어는 주어에 따라 be동사를 다르게 써줘야 해요. 주어에 따라 모양이 변하는 거랍니다. 모양은 서로 다르지만 세 가지(am, is, are) 모두 다 주어를 '설명'해 주는 역할을 합니다. 우리말로 '~이다'라는 뜻이에요.

3. be동사의 부정문은 어떻게 만들어요?

우리말로 '~가 아니다'라는 의미를 영어로 말하고 싶을 때는 be동사 바로 뒤에 not을 붙여서 부정문을 만들어요.

Positives (긍정)			Negatives (부정)			
인칭대명사	Be	축약형	인칭대명사	Be		축약형
I	am	I'm	I	am		I'm not
You	are	You're	You	are	Not	You aren't
He / She / It	is	He's / She's / It's	He / She / It	is		He(She / It) isn't
We / They	are	We're / They're	We / They	are		We(They) aren't

Go for it!

A. Match and write *am*, *is*, or *are*.

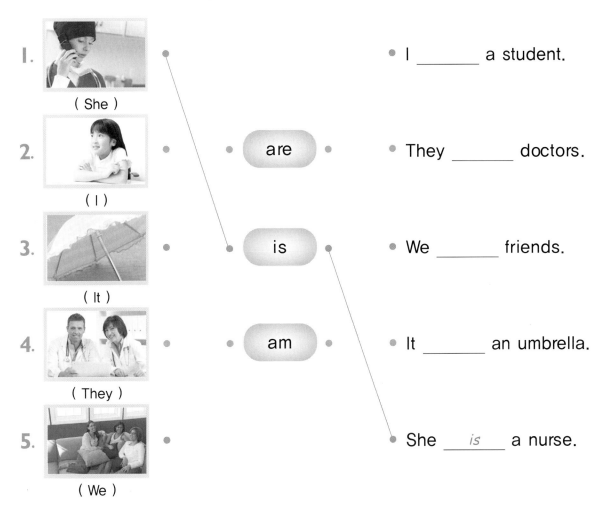

1. (She)

2. (I)

3. (It)

4. (They)

5. (We)

are

is

am

I _____ a student.

They _____ doctors.

We _____ friends.

It _____ an umbrella.

She ___*is*___ a nurse.

B. Write the contractions.

1. He is → _____*He's*_____

2. He is not → _____

3. I am → _____

4. I am not → _____

5. She is → _____

6. She is not → _____

7. You are → _____

8. You are not → _____

9. We are → _____

10. We are not → _____

11. They are → _____

12. They are not → _____

13. It is → _____

14. It is not → _____

C. Rewrite the sentences into the plural.

1. I am a student. → *We are students* .

2. It is a box. → _____ .

3. She is a doctor. → _____ .

4. He is a farmer. → _____ .

5. You are a teacher. → _____ .

D. Make negative sentences using the given words.

1. He is old. → *He isn't young* . (young)

2. She is a doctor. → _____ . (nurse)

3. They are tall. → _____ . (short)

4. We are happy. → _____ . (sad)

5. It is an elephant. → _____ . (ant)

6. You are handsome. → _____ . (ugly)

7. I am 11 years old. → _____ . (10)

Grammar in Writing

A. Look at the photos and write sentences.

1.

(not / train / it)

➡️ *It isn't a train.* .

2.

(it / zebra)

➡️ _____ .

3.

(they / cat)

➡️ _____ .

4.

(painter / she)

➡️ _____ .

5.

(not / happy / we)

➡️ _____ .

6.

(not / pig / it)

➡️ _____ .

B. Look, circle and write.

1.

(It / (They)) ➡️ (is / (are) / am)

➡️ *They are dolphins* .

(dolphin)

2.

(She / He) ➡️ (is / are / am)

➡️ _____ .

(English teacher)

unit 2 Be + S ~ ?

Grammar focus

Q: **Is** he a pilot?

A: (긍정) Yes, he is.　　　(부정) No, he isn't.

1. be동사의 의문문은 어떻게 만드나요?

be동사의 의문문은 be동사를 문장 맨 앞으로 보내고, 문장 마지막에 물음표(?)를 붙이기만 하면 돼요.

2. 답은 어떻게 하나요?

Yes나 No로 답하고 동사는 주어에 맞게 be동사를 써서 대답하면 돼요. Yes로 대답할 때는 축약형을 쓰지 않는다는 것도 알아두세요.

Questions	Answers	
Am I ~?	Yes, you are.	No, you aren't.
Are you ~?	Yes, I am.	No, I'm not.
Is he / she / it ~?	Yes, he / she / it is.	No, he / she / it isn't.
Are we ~?	Yes, you are.	No, you aren't.
Are you ~?	Yes, we are.	No, we aren't.
Are they ~?	Yes, they are.	No, they aren't.

Usage

She is a violinist.

➡ Q: **Is** she a violinist?

A: **Yes**, she is.

They are tigers.

➡ Q: **Are** they tigers?

A: **No**, they aren't.

Go for it!

A. Circle the correct word.

1. (**Is** / Are) it a school?

2. (Is / Are) they insects?

3. (Is / Are) they zebras?

4. (Is / Are) you hungry?

5. (Is / Am) I a police officer?

6. (Is / Are) he a doctor?

7. (Is / Are) she a painter?

8. (Is / Are) they socks?

9. (Is / Are) it a frog?

10. (Is / Are) they baseball players?

B. Read and write *Am, Is* or *Are*.

1. ___*Are*___ the children happy?

2. _____ she a teacher?

3. _____ he a tennis player?

4. _____ you sad?

5. _____ she an actress?

6. _____ he an actor?

7. _____ they dancers?

8. _____ they soldiers?

9. _____ we students?

10. _____ it a panda?

C. Fill in the blanks.

Questions	Positives (Yes)	Negatives (No)
1. _Am_ I a nurse?	Yes, _you_ _are_ .	No, _you_ _aren't_ .
2. _____ you a dancer?	Yes, _____ _____ .	No, _____ _____ .
3. _____ he a dentist?	Yes, _____ _____ .	No, _____ _____ .
4. _____ she a soldier?	Yes, _____ _____ .	No, _____ _____ .
5. _____ it a panda?	Yes, _____ _____ .	No, _____ _____ .
6. _____ you singers?	Yes, _____ _____ .	No, _____ _____ .
7. _____ they happy?	Yes, _____ _____ .	No, _____ _____ .

D. Check the correct answer.

1. Is he a cook?
   - ☑ Yes, he is.
   - ☐ Yes, he are

2. Are they shoes?
   - ☐ No, they aren't.
   - ☐ Yes, they are.

3. Is she a painter?
   - ☐ Yes, it is.
   - ☐ Yes, she is.

Grammar in Writing

A. Look and fill in the blanks.

1.

   <u>Is</u> <u>it</u> the Statue of Liverty?
   <u>Yes</u> , <u>it</u> <u>is</u> .

2.

   _____ _____ a puppy?
   _____ , _____ _____ .

3.

   _____ _____ a pilot? (he)
   _____ , _____ _____ .

4.

   _____ _____ a baseball player? (she)
   _____ , _____ _____ .

B. Write questions and answers.

1.

   (soldier)
   Q: Is he a pilot?
   A: <u>No, he isn't</u> . <u>He is a soldier</u> .

2.

   (duck)
   Q: Is it a cheetah?
   A: _____ . _____ .

3.

   (in the classroom)
   Q: Are they at the park?
   A: _____ .
   _____ .

4.

   (bear)
   Q: Are they elephants?
   A: _____ .
   _____ .

Whose + ⓝ ~ ?

Grammar focus

Q: **Whose** skateboard is that?
A: It's Kevin's skateboard.

1. **Whose는 어떨 때 쓰는 거예요?**
   '~은 누구의 것입니까?'의 뜻으로 소유에 대해 묻는 말이에요.

2. **대답은 어떻게 하나요?**
   누구의 것인지를 물어보는 말이므로 〈소유격＋명사〉, 소유대명사 또는 사람 이름의 소유격으로 대답해요. Tom과 같이 사람 이름의 소유격은 명사에 -'s를 붙여서 만들어요.

Wh-Questions	Answers with Possessive Nouns
Whose book is this? Whose book is that?	It's Kevin's book. It's his book. It's his.
Whose books are these? Whose books are those?	They're Nancy's books. They're her books. They're hers.

Usage

Q: **Whose** cat is this?
A: It is Sunny's cat.

Q: **Whose** kite is that?
A: It is Scott's kite.

Q: **Whose** flowers are these?
A: They are Jessica's flowers.

Q: **Whose** T-shirts are those?
A: They are Bob's T-shirts.

Go for it!

A. Combine the words.

1. bag / Kevin   →   *Kevin's bag*

2. hat / Mary   →   _____

3. house / Bob   →   _____

4. tail / a dog   →   _____

5. car / Laura   →   _____

6. books / Ron   →   _____

B. Circle the correct word and write.

1.

   (**Erika's** / hers)

   Q: Whose violin is that?
   A: It's ___*Erica's*___ violin.

2.

   (her / hers)

   Q: Whose ball is this?
   A: It's _____ ball.

3.

   (my / mine)

   Q: Whose shoes are these?
   A: They're _____.

C. Read and circle the correct word.

1.

   Q: (Who / What / Whose) is he?
   A: He is Ben Thomas.

2.

   Q: (Who / What / Whose) bicycle is that?
   A: It's Sandra's bicycle.

3.

   Q: (Who / What / Whose) is it?
   A: It is a watch.

4.

   Q: (Who / What / Whose) house is that?
   A: It's Kevin's house.

D. Look at the table and complete the sentences.

Brian(husband, dad)

Karen(wife, mom)

＊Brian and Karen are married. They have a son, Eric, and a daughter, Julia.

Eric(son, brother)

Julia(daughter, sister)

1. Brian – husband　　➔　*Brain is Karen's husband*　　.
2. Karen – wife　　➔　_____.
3. Eric – brother　　➔　_____.
4. Julia – sister　　➔　_____.
5. Eric – son　　➔　_____.

38

Grammar in Writing

A. Read and complete answers.

1. Q: Is this your book?
   A: No, _it isn't_ . _It is Kevin's book_ . (Kevin)

2. Q: Are these her skates?
   A: No, _____ . _____ . (Bob)

3. Q: Is that his car?
   A: No, _____ . _____ . (Nancy)

4. Q: Are those his glasses?
   A: No, _____ . _____ . (Susan)

5. Q: Is that your shopping bag?
   A: No, _____ . _____ . (Karen)

B. Read and make dialogues.

1. A: Is this your pencil?
   B: No, it isn't.
   A: _Whose pencil is this_ ?
   B: _It's Lucy's pencil_ . (Lucy)

2. A: Are these his jackts?
   B: No, they aren't.
   A: _____ ?
   B: _____ . (Jason)

3. A: Is that her laptop?
   B: No, it isn't.
   A: _____ ?
   B: _____ . (John)

4. A: Are those my books?
   B: No, they aren't.
   A: _____ ?
   B: _____ . (Sara)

What time & How ~?

Q: **What time** is it now?
A: It is **two** o'clock.

Q: **How** is she?
A: She is **happy**.

1. What time ~이 뭐예요?
시간을 물어볼 때 사용하는 말이에요.

2. How는 언제 쓰는 건가요?
궁금한 것이 사람의 감정 상태일 때 How를 be동사 앞에 써요. '~은 어떻습니까?'라는 뜻이에요.

TIME(시간)		People's feeling(감정)	
Question	Answers	Questions	Answers
What time is it?	It's ten o'clock.	How are you?	I am happy.
		How is he?	He is sad.
	It's four thirty.	How is she?	She is angry.
		How are they?	They are tired.

Usage

Q: **What time** is it?
A: It's **eight twenty**.

Q: **How** is he?
A: He is **tired**.

Go for it!

A. Look and check.

1. What time is it?

- ☑ It's one fifty-five.
- ☐ It's two o'clock.

2. What time is it?

- ☐ It's ten o'clock.
- ☐ It's nine o'clock.

3. What time is it?

- ☐ It's a half past six.
- ☐ It's a half past seven.

4. What time is it?

- ☐ It's five fifteen.
- ☐ It's a half past five.

B. Read and choose.

1.

Q: How (is he / are she)?
A: He is sad.

2.

Q: How (are they / is she)?
A: She is angry.

3.

Q: How (are they / is she)?
A: They are happy.

4.

Q: How (is you / are you)?
A: I am sleepy.

C. Look and match.

1. `2:30` •
2. `9:45` •
3. `6:55` •
4. `4:20` •
5. `10:30` •

• It's four twenty.
• It's nine forty-five.
• It' a half past ten.
• It's a half past two.
• It's six fifty-five.

C. Look, choose and write.

| happy | tired | angry |

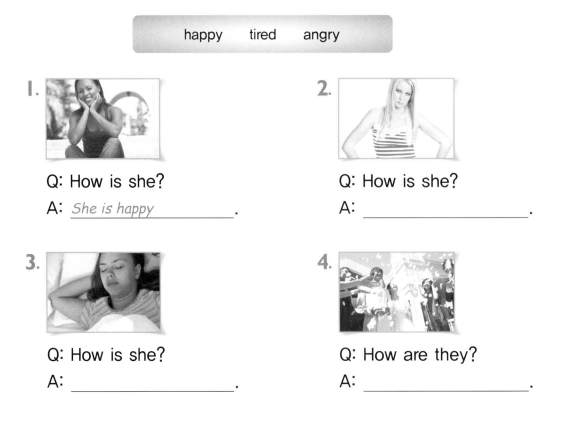

1.
Q: How is she?
A: *She is happy* .

2.
Q: How is she?
A: _____ .

3.
Q: How is she?
A: _____ .

4.
Q: How are they?
A: _____ .

Grammar in Writing

A. Look and make questions.

1.

Q: *How is she* _____?
A: She is happy.

2.

Q: _____?
A: They are angry.

3.

Q: _____?
A: They are sad.

4.

Q: _____?
A: He is tired.

B. Read and make dialogues.

1. A: Is it ten o'clock?
   B: No, it isn't.
   A: *What time is it* _____?
   B: *It's ten twenty-five* _____. (10:25)

2. A: Is it seven o'clock?
   B: No, it isn't.
   A: _____?
   B: _____. (7:50)

3. A: Is it two o'clock?
   B: No, it isn't.
   A: _____?
   B: _____. (9:30)

Chapter 3
The Simple Present

S+Ⓥ

Grammar focus

She is a doctor.
She works in a hospital.
She sees sick people.

1. 일반동사가 뭐예요?

   일반 동사는 '먹다, 자다, 가다, 앉다, 운동하다, 공부하다'라는 우리말처럼 이 세상에 있는 모든 움직임이나, 동작을 나타내는 말이에요.

2. 어떤 동사에는 왜 -s나 -es가 붙어있죠?

   영어에는 주어가 3인칭 단수(He / She / It)일 때 동사에 -(e)s를 붙이자는 약속이 있어요.

대부분의 동사 ⇒ -s를 붙임	-sh, -ch, -x, -s로 끝나는 동사 ⇒ -es 붙임	〈자음+y〉로 끝나는 동사 ⇒ y를 i로 바꾸고 -es 붙임
come ➡ comes	watch ➡ watches	study ➡ studies
read ➡ reads	brush ➡ brushes	fly ➡ flies
eat ➡ eats	fix ➡ fixes	cry ➡ cries
drink ➡ drinks	kiss ➡ kisses	worry ➡ worries

Usage

I study Korean.
She studies Korean.

I watch TV.
He watches TV.

I brush my teeth.
She brushes her teeth.

I swim.
She swims.

I cry all day.
The baby cries all day.

Go for it!

A. Look and circle.

	I / You / We / They	He / She / It
1.	rain	(raines / (rains))
2.	speak	(speaks / speakies)
3.	cry	(crys / cries)
4.	laugh	(laughs / laughes)
5.	teach	(teachs / teaches)
6.	brush	(brushes / brushs)
7.	help	(helps / helpes)
8.	eat	(eats / eaies)
9.	sleep	(sleepes / sleeps)
10.	play	(plays / plaies)
11.	enjoy	(enjoys / enjoies)
12.	fly	(flys / flies)
13.	kiss	(kisss / kisses)

B. Change the verb form.

1. I watch → She _watches_

2. We brush → He _____

3. I catch → She _____

4. We mix → He _____

5. I study → She _____

6. We cry → He _____

7. I wash → She _____

8. We fly → He _____

9. I fix → She _____

10. We kiss → He _____

C. Match and write.

1.

He _reads_ a newspaper.
(read)

2.

She _____ her hair.
(brush)

3.

The man _____ students.
(teach)

4.

The bird _____ in the sky.
(fly)

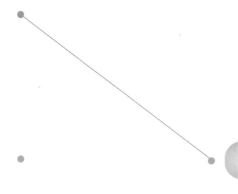

+ -s

+ -es

+ -ies

Grammar in Writing

A. Rewrite the sentences.

1. I brush my teeth. ➔ She _____*brushes her teeth*_____ .

2. We drink milk every morning. ➔ He _____ .

3. Tom studies English. ➔ Tom and I _____ .

4. They wash their hands. ➔ She _____ .

5. They catch the baseball. ➔ My cat _____ .

6. I finish my homework. ➔ He _____ .

B. Look at the chart and write.

	Every morning	Every afternoon	Every evening
Susan and Bob	wake up at 6:30	eat lunch at 12:00	go to bed at 10:00
Susan	brush her teeth	study English	listen to music
Bob	wash his hands	play soccer	watch TV

1. Susan and Bob _____*wake up at 6:30*_____ every morning.

2. Susan _____*brushes her teeth*_____ every morning.

3. Bob _____ every morning.

4. Susan and Bob _____ every afternoon.

5. Susan _____ every afternoon.

6. Bob _____ every afternoon.

7. Susan and Bob _____ every evening.

8. Bob _____ every evening.

9. Susan _____ every evening.

S+don't[doesn't]+Ⓥ

Grammar focus

He is a pianist.
He **plays** the piano.
He **doesn't play** the violin.

1. 부정문은 어떻게 만드나요?

동사 앞에 don't를 붙이면 '~하지 않다, ~가 아니다'의 의미의 부정문이 되는 거예요.

2. 왜 don't를 쓰지 않고 doesn't를 쓰나요?

주어가 3인칭 단수(He / She / It / Tom..)일 때 일반동사 앞에 doesn't(=does not)를 써요. 이 때 도우미 역할을 하는 does가 3인칭 단수임을 알리는 일을 하기 때문에 일반 동사는 모양을 바꾸지 않고 동사원형 그대로 써야 해요.

Affirmative(긍정)				Negative(부정)			
I You We They	drink	He She It Tom	drinks	I You We They	don't drink	He She It Mary	doesn't drink

＊do not(=don't) / does not(=doesn't)은 축약형을 많이 써요.

Usage

I **don't like** vegetables.
I like a hamburger.

We **don't play** soccer.
We play basketball.

They **don't ride** a bus.
They walk to school.

He **doesn't drink** coffee.
He drinks juice.

She **doesn't watch** TV.
She reads books.

It **doesn't fly**.
It swims.

Go for it!

A. Read and write.

	Positives	Negatives
1.	I like apples.	I *don't like apples* .
2.	You like books.	You _____ .
3.	He likes her.	He _____ .
4.	She likes you.	She _____ .
5.	It likes the food.	It _____ .
6.	We like oranges.	We _____ .
7.	They like kiwis.	They _____ .

B. Circle the correct word.

1.

We (doesn't / don't) study.

2.

They (don't / doesn't) play baseball.

3.

She (don't / doesn't) wake up early.

4.

He (doesn't / don't) want the car.

C. Correct the mistakes.

1. She don't like Japanese.
   → She _____ *doesn't like Japanese* _____ .

2. You doesn't want the apple.
   → You _____ .

3. She don't eat hamburgers.
   → She _____ .

4. He don't watch TV.
   → He _____ .

5. They doesn't play computer games.
   → They _____ .

6. Jessica don't cry.
   → Jessica _____ .

D. Make positives and negatives.

1. like / I / oranges
   → (P) *I like oranges* _____ .
   → (N) *I don't like oranges* _____ .

2. study / Nancy / Korean
   → (P) _____ .
   → (N) _____ .

3. read / Peter / books
   → (P) _____ .
   → (N) _____ .

4. brush / she / her hair
   → (P) _____ .
   → (N) _____ .

Grammar in Writing

A. Look and write the sentences using the given information.

ride a car (X)

1. I _____don't ride a car_____ .
   I _____ride a bicycle_____ .

ride a bicycle (O)

drink coffee (X)

2. She _____ .
   She _____ .

drink milk (O)

play soccer (X)

3. He _____ .
   He _____ .

play baseball (O)

study English (X)

4. Laura _____ .
   Laura _____ .

study Russian (O)

B. Make the sentences negative.

1. She / play / the guitar
   ➡ _She doesn't play the guitar_ .

2. He / like / chocolate
   ➡ _____ .

3. We / eat / hamburgers
   ➡ _____ .

4. They / drink / coffee
   ➡ _____ .

Do[Does] + S + Ⓥ ~ ?

Grammar focus

Q: **Does** she jog every morning?
A: Yes, she **does**.
Q: **Does** she listen to music?
A: No, she **doesn't**.

1. 의문문은 어떻게 만들어요?

문장 맨 앞에 Do를 쓰고 문장 끝에 물음표(?)를 붙이기만 하면 돼요. 주어가 3인칭 단수인 경우에만 Does를 써요. '~하니, ~이니?'라는 의미예요.

2. 답은 어떻게 하나요?

be동사와 마찬가지로 일반동사의 의문문도 Yes나 No로 대답하는 거예요. 긍정일 때는 〈Yes, 주어+ do(does)〉, 부정일 때는 〈No, 주어+don't(doesn't)〉로 짧게 대답해요.

Q	Do you ~ ?　　　Do we~? Do they ~ ?　　Do I ~ ?	Does he ~ ?　　　Does she ~ ? Does it ~ ?
A	Yes, I do. / No, I don't.	Yes, she does. / No, she doesn't.

Usage

Q: **Do** you study English?
A: Yes, I **do**.

Q: **Do** they play baseball?
A: No, they **don't**.

Q: **Does** she brush her teeth?
A: Yes, she **does**.

Q: **Does** he drink orange juice?
A: No, he **doesn't**.

Go for it!

A. Circle the correct word.

1. (Do / **Does**) Tom drink milk every day?

2. (Do / Does) your brother walk to school?

3. (Do / Does) they like English?

4. (Do / Does) Bob love her?

5. (Do / Does) Scott drive a taxi?

6. (Do / Does) the children play soccer?

7. (Do / Does) they speak English in class?

8. (Do / Does) they eat breakfast every day?

9. (Do / Does) you know Jane and Tom?

B. Write *Does* or *Do*.

1. _____*Do*_____ you speak English?

2. _____ Peter listen to music?

3. _____ the children walk to school?

4. _____ we get up early?

5. _____ Bob watch TV?

6. _____ Nancy like horror movies?

7. _____ Lucy take a shower?

8. _____ your sister play the piano?

C. Look and complete the sentences.

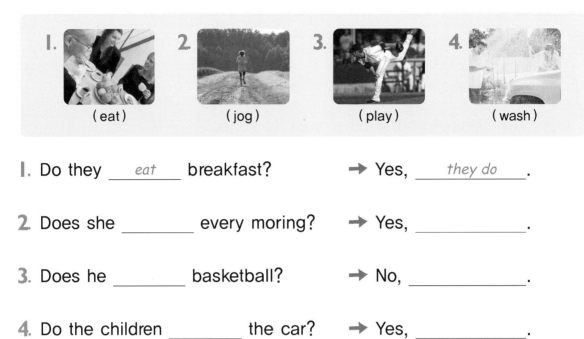

| 1. (eat) | 2. (jog) | 3. (play) | 4. (wash) |

1. Do they ___eat___ breakfast? → Yes, ___they do___ .

2. Does she _____ every moring? → Yes, _____ .

3. Does he _____ basketball? → No, _____ .

4. Do the children _____ the car? → Yes, _____ .

D. Write a question. Then, write a negative sentence.

1. Scott likes green tea.
   → *Does Scott like green tea*_____?
   → *Scott doesn't like green tea*_____.

2. Frogs cry in the pond.
   → _____?
   → _____.

3. He swims in the pool.
   → _____?
   → _____.

Grammar in Writing

A. Look at the chart and make questions and answers.

	I	He	She	They
live in Seattle	O	X	O	O
play the guitar	X	O	X	X
like hiking	O	X	O	X
speak Korean very well	X	O	X	O
teach English	X	O	X	X
eat carrots	O	X	O	X

1. I / live in Seattle

   → *Do you live in Seattle* ? *Yes, I do* .

2. She / play the guitar

   → _____ ? _____ .

3. They / like hiking

   → _____ ? _____ .

4. He / speak Korean very well

   → _____ ? _____ .

5. She / teach English

   → _____ ? _____ .

6. I / eat carrots

   → _____ ? _____ .

7. They / eat carrots

   → _____ ? _____ .

8. She / live in Seattle

   → _____ ? _____ .

unit 4 S+have[has] ~ / What ~?

Grammar focus

She **has** many books.
She **does** her homework.

Q: **What** does he do?
A: He does **exercises**.

1. 불규칙 동사가 뭐예요?

3인칭 단수 주어의 경우, 동사에 보통 규칙적으로 -e 또는 -es를 붙이는데, 불규칙 동사는 특별한 규칙이 없이 변하게 돼요.

have ➡ has　　　go ➡ goes　　　do ➡ does

2. 의문문에서 일반동사는 왜 모양이 변하지 않고 동사원형을 그대로 쓰나요?

의문문에서는 문장 맨 앞에 있는 Does가 3인칭 단수임을 알려주는 역할을 하기 때문에 동사원형인 have, go, do를 그대로 쓰는 거예요.

3. what으로 시작하는 의문문은 어떻게 만드나요?

〈What+do/does+주어+동사원형~?〉의 어순으로 만들어요. Yes나 No로 대답할 수 없어요.

What (무엇을, 무엇이)	do does	주어 + 동사원형 ~ ?

Usage

Q: **Does** she **have** a cell phone?
A: No, she doesn't. She **has** a laptop.

Q: **What** does she eat?
A: She eats **French Fries**.

Go for it!

A. Read and circle.

1. Q: Does she (has / (have)) a puppy?
   A: Yes, she ((does) / has).

2. Q: What (do / does) he like?
   A: (Yes, he does. / He likes books.)

3. Q: Does he (goes / go) to church every Sunday?
   A: No, he (don't / doesn't).

4. Q: What (do / does) they drink?
   A: They (drinks / drink) milk and juice.

B. Match and write.

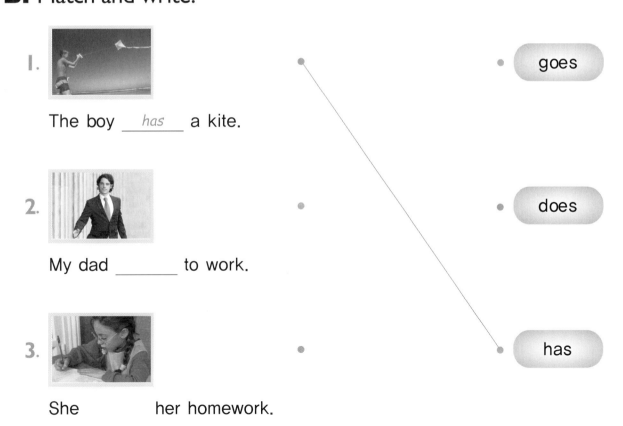

1. The boy __*has*__ a kite.

2. My dad _____ to work.

3. She _____ her homework.

goes

does

has

C. Make questions.

1. She / want / what   ➡   *What does she want* _____ ?

2. He / eat / what   ➡   _____ ?

3. They / like / what   ➡   _____ ?

4. You / teach / what   ➡   _____ ?

5. She / make / what   ➡   _____ ?

6. The dog / drink / what   ➡   _____ ?

D. Read and make questions.

1. I go to the museum every Saturday.
   ➡ *Do you go to the museum every Saturday* _____ ?

2. Tiffany has many friends.
   ➡ _____ ?

3. Bob does his homework every evening.
   ➡ _____ ?

4. She has dinner at home every day.
   ➡ _____ ?

5. Kelly and Peter do the housework every Sunday.
   ➡ _____ ?

Grammar in Writing

A. Look at the table and make dialogues.

	play the piano	make cookies	enjoy skiing	like cheeseburgers
Jessica	O	X	O	O
Nancy	X	O	X	O
Bob and Kathy	X	O	O	X

1. A: Does Jessica play the guitar?
   B: No, *she doesn't* .
   A: *What does she play* ?
   B: *She plays the piano* .

2. A: Does Nancy make cakes?
   B: No, _____ .
   A: _____ ?
   B: _____ .

3. A: Do Bob and Kathy enjoy skating?
   B: No, _____ .
   A: _____ ?
   B: _____ .

4. A: Does Jessica like pizza?
   B: No, _____ .
   A: _____ ?
   B: _____ .

5. A: Does Nancy like hamburgers?
   B: No, _____ .
   A: _____ ?
   B: _____ .

6. A: Do Bob and Kathy make juice?
   B: No, _____ .
   A: _____ ?
   B: _____ .

Do[Don't / Be] ~

Grammar focus

(At school the teacher says:)
Open your books.
Be quiet!
Don't talk in class.
Don't sleep in class.

1. 명령문이 뭐예요?

명령문은 우리말로 '숙제해라', '공부해라', '조용히 해라'처럼 상대방에게 명령하거나 부탁할 때 쓰는 문장이에요. 주어(you)를 생략하고 동사원형으로 시작해요.

2. 부정명령문은 어떻게 만드나요?

부정명령문은 문장 맨 앞에 Don't를 붙여서 만들어요. be동사도 앞에 Don't을 붙여 우리말로 '~하지 마라'의 부정명령 표현을 만들어요.

Positive(긍정)	Negative(부정)
Sit down.	Don't sit down.
Stand up.	Don't stand up.
Open the window.	Don't eat too much.
Do your homework.	Don't be afraid.
Be careful.	Don't be late.

Usage

Do your homework. **Brush** your teeth. **Don't watch** TV. **Don't be** afraid.

Go for it!

A. Circle the correct word.

1.

   ((Don't) / Be) cry.

2.

   (Don't / Be) quiet in class.

3.

   Don't (eat / eats) chocolate too much.

4.

   (Drink / Be) your milk.

B. Write the opposite.

1. Sing a song. → *Don't sing a song* .

2. Drink this orange juice. → _____ .

3. Don't swim in the pool. → _____ .

4. Don't read this book. → _____ .

5. Don't listen to your teacher. → _____ .

6. Climb the tree. → _____ .

C. Choose and write.

A typical day in Scott's life

wake up	don't forget	eat	put on

1 In the morning my mom says:

1. _____*Wake up*_____ ! It's seven o'clock!
2. _____ your breakfast.
3. _____ your bag.
4. _____ your jacket.

be	don't talk	hand in	don't use

2 At school my teacher says:

5. _____ your cell phone.
6. _____ quiet.
7. _____ your homework.
8. _____ with your friends.

do	turn off	go

3 In the evening my dad says:

9. _____ the TV!
10. _____ your homework.
11. _____ to bed early.

Grammar in Writing

A. Change the sentences into positive(P) and negative(N) imperatives.

1. You drink much water.
   (P) *Drink much water* . (N) *Don't drink much water* .

2. You are afraid of the cat.
   (P) _____ . (N) _____ .

3. You are quite during the class.
   (P) _____ . (N) _____ .

4. You read a book every day.
   (P) _____ . (N) _____ .

5. You eat the hamburger.
   (P) _____ . (N) _____ .

B. Read and complete the sentences.

1.

   You are in the class. (quiet)
   ___*Be quiet*___ during the class.

2.

   The movie is starting. (turn off)
   _____ your cell phone.

3.

   It's cold outside. (go out)
   _____ .

4.

   Your are on the plane. (smoke)
   _____ here.

Chapter 4

The Present Continuous

Unit 1. **S** + **be** + Ⓥ-ing

Unit 2. **S** + **be not** + Ⓥ-ing

Unit 3. **B**e + **S** + Ⓥ-ing?

Unit 4. **W**hat + **be** + **S** + Ⓥ-ing?

unit 1 S + be + Ⓥ -ing

Grammar focus

The children **are sitting** on the sofa.
They **are watching** TV.

1. 현재 진행형이 뭐예요?

진행형은 지금 보고 있는 순간에 진행 중인 동작이나 행동을 말하는 거예요. 〈be동사(am, is, are)+Ⓥ-ing〉의 형태로 만들고 '~하고 있다, ~ 하고 있는 중이다'라는 뜻이 됩니다.

2. 진행형은 어떻게 만드나요?

❶ 대부분의 동사원형에 -ing를 붙여요.

go ➡ going   eat ➡ eating   work ➡ working
see ➡ seeing   teach ➡ teaching   do ➡ doing

❷ -e로 끝나는 동사는 -e를 지우고 -ing를 붙여요.

take ➡ taking   come ➡ coming   live ➡ living   make ➡ making

❸ 〈단모음+단자음〉으로 끝나는 동사는 마지막 자음철자를 한 번 더 쓰고 -ing를 붙여요.

sit ➡ sitting   swim ➡ swimming   run ➡ running

Usage

I **am** listen**ing** to music.

We **are** read**ing** a book.

He **is** wash**ing** his hands.

She **is** study**ing**.

They **are** runn**ing**.

Go for it!

A. Read and fill in the blanks.

1. He is ___playing___ the piano. (play)

2. They are _____. (swim)

3. She is _____ the door. (paint)

4. We are _____ dinner. (have)

5. You are _____. (run)

6. Tom is _____. (sleep)

7. The girl is _____ a book. (read)

B. Correct the mistakes.

1. I am run.   ➡ _I am running_____.

2. We is playing soccer.   ➡ _____.

3. She is siting on the bench.   ➡ _____.

4. You are makeing a cake.   ➡ _____.

5. They is walk to school.   ➡ _____.

C. Look and write.

	I			He / Tom / Kevin	
	Base verb	be + Ⓥ-ing		Base verb	be + Ⓥ-ing
1.	see	*am seeing*	2.	write	*is writing*
3.	swim	_____	4.	begin	_____
5.	work	_____	6.	sit	_____

	She / Susan / Lucy			They / You / We	
	Base verb	be + Ⓥ-ing		Base verb	be + Ⓥ-ing
7.	make	_____	8.	listen	_____
9.	come	_____	10.	have	_____
11.	run	_____	12.	do	_____
13.	stop	_____	14.	live	_____
15.	study	_____	16.	go	_____

Grammar in Writing

A. Read and fill in the blanks.

1.

Steve _is reading_ a newspaper.
(read)

2.

He _____ his hands.
(wash)

3.

They _____ for a bus.
(wait)

4.

She _____ to music.
(listen)

B. Look and write.

1.

(play / the violin)

What is Karen doing?

→ _She is playing the violin_____.

2.

(brush / her teeth)

What is Nancy doing?

→ _____.

3.

(study / in the library)

What are they doing?

→ _____.

Grammar focus

He **isn't singing**. (=He's not singing.)
She **isn't singing**. (=She's not singing.)
They**'re dancing**.

1. 진행형의 부정문은 어떻게 만드나요?

   진행형의 부정문은 '~하고 있지 않다'라는 의미로 주어가 단수이든 복수이든 관계없이 be동사 뒤에 'not'을 붙여 만들어요.

be + Ⓥ-ing	be + not + Ⓥ-ing
I'm working	I'm not working.
You're / We're / They're working.	You / We / They aren't working.
She's / He's / It's working	She / He / It isn't working.

Usage

I'm not wash**ing** my face.
I'm brushing my teeth.

They **aren't** sleep**ing**.
They're watching TV.

He **isn't** listen**ing** to music.
He's drinking milk.

She **isn't** wear**ing** glasses.
She's wearing a hat.

Go for it!

A. Make the sentences negative.

1. I'm walking now. ➡ *I'm not walking now* .

2. You're singing now. ➡ _____ .

3. We're dancing now. ➡ _____ .

4. He's studying now. ➡ _____ .

5. She's sleeping now. ➡ _____ .

6. It's raining now. ➡ _____ .

7. They're running now. ➡ _____ .

B. Make the sentences negative.

1. She / read / a book / not ➡ *She isn't reading a book* .

2. You / watch / a movie / not ➡ _____ .

3. It / climb / a tree / not ➡ _____ .

4. I / drink / juice / not ➡ _____ .

5. They / walk / to school / not ➡ _____ .

C. Match and write.

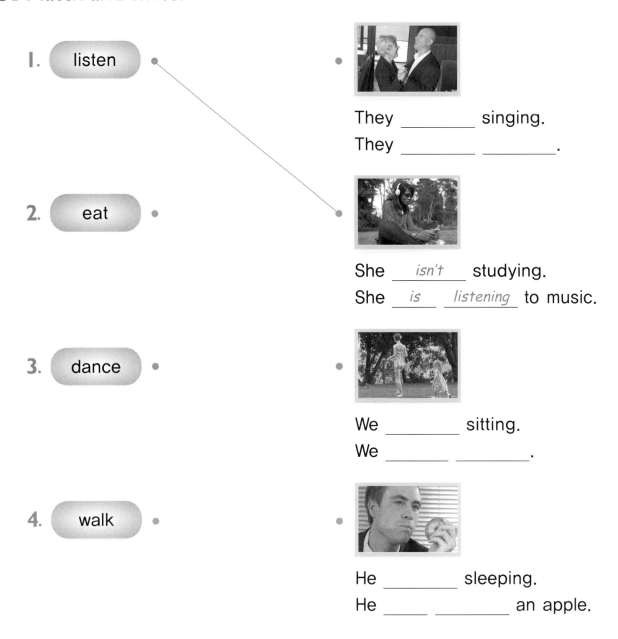

1. listen

They _____ singing.
They _____ _____.

2. eat

She ___isn't___ studying.
She ___is___ ___listening___ to music.

3. dance

We _____ sitting.
We _____ _____.

4. walk

He _____ sleeping.
He _____ _____ an apple.

D. Put the words in the correct order.

1. He ___*isn't reading a book*___.
   (reading / a book / isn't)

2. Rachel _____.
   (the drum / playing / isn't)

Grammar in Writing

A. Make positives and negatives.

1. Lucy sleeps. ➡ (P) *Lucy is sleeping* .
   (N) *Lucy isn't sleeping* .

2. My sister does her homework. ➡ (P) _____ .
   (N) _____ .

3. She sits on the bench. ➡ (P) _____ .
   (N) _____ .

4. Peter drinks water. ➡ (P) _____ .
   (N) _____ .

5. They play tennis. ➡ (P) _____ .
   (N) _____ .

B. Look and write.

1.	2.	3.
walk (X) / run (O)	eat (X) / wash (O)	cook (X) / brush (O)

1. They _____ *aren't walking* _____ to school.
   They _____ *are running* _____ to school.

2. Bob _____ pizza.
   Bob _____ his face.

3. Kelly _____ dinner.
   Kelly _____ her teeth.

Be + S + Ⓥ-ing?

Grammar focus

Q: **Is** she play**ing** soccer?
A: **No**, **she isn't**.
Q: **Is** she play**ing** tennis?
A: **Yes, she is**.

1. 진행형의 의문문은 어떻게 만드나요?

'~하고 있니, 하는 중이니?'라는 의문문을 만들고 싶을 때는 〈주어+be+Ⓥ-ing〉의 형태에서 be동사만 문장 맨 앞으로 보내고 물음표(?)를 써주면 돼요.

2. 답은 어떻게 하나요?

대답은 Yes나 No로 하고, 긍정일 때는 〈Yes, 주어+be동사〉, 부정일 때는 〈No, 주어+be not〉으로 대답해요. 대답의 주어는 의문문에 있는 주어를 알맞은 대명사로 바꾸어 사용하면 됩니다.

Be verb+subject+Ⓥ-ing ~?			
Q: Are you singing?	Q: Is he walking?	Q: Is she dancing?	Q: Are they working?
A: Yes, I am.	A: Yes, he is.	A: Yes, she is.	A: Yes, they are.
No, I'm not.	No, he isn't.	No, she isn't.	No, they aren't.

Usage

Q: **Is** she dan**cing**?
A: Yes, she is.

Q: **Is** he eat**ing** pizza?
A: No, he isn't. He is eating a hamburger.

Q: **Are** they go**ing** to school?
A: Yes, they are.

Q: **Are** you work**ing**?
A: No, I'm not. I am sleeping.

Go for it!

A. Circle the correct word.

1.
(**Is** / are) she reading a newspaper?

2.
(Is / Are) he playing the piano?

3.
(Are / Is) they watching a movie?

4.
(Am / Is) Tom painting the house?

5.
(Is / Are) the man doing exercises?

6.
(Is / Are) Kelly and Susan singing?

B. Read and write answers.

1. Q: Is he talking on the phone?   A: Yes, _____*he is*_____.

2. Q: Are they having lunch?   A: No, _____.

3. Q: Is Peter doing his homework?   A: Yes, _____.

4. Q: Is Laura reading a book?   A: No, _____.

5. Q: Are the dogs drinking water?   A: Yes, _____.

6. Q: Are Tom and Bob sleeping?   A: No, _____.

C. Look and make questions.

1.
(they / walk)

Q: *Are they walking* ?

2.
(Nancy / sleep)

Q: _____ ?

3.
(they / sit on the sofa)

Q: _____ ?

4.
(she / play the guitar)

Q: _____ ?

D. Fill in the blanks.

1. ___Is___ Sunny drinking coffee? → Yes, ___she is___ .

2. _____ he swimming? → No, _____ .

3. _____ your mom cooking? → Yes, _____ .

4. _____ your friends singing? → No, _____ .

5. _____ they smiling? → Yes, _____ .

6. _____ you doing your homework? → No, _____ .

Grammar in Writing

A. Make questions and answers.

1. The man is crying.
   Q: *Is the man crying* _____ ?
   A: *Yes, he is* _____ . *No, he isn't* _____ .

2. She is sitting on the chair.
   Q: _____ ?
   A: _____ . _____ .

3. The boy is flying a kite.
   Q: _____ ?
   A: _____ . _____ .

4. They are learning yoga.
   Q: _____ ?
   A: _____ . _____ .

B. Look at the pictures. Write questions and answers.

1. (she / run / ? ➡ No / walk)
   Q: *Is she running* _____ ?
   A: *No, she isn't. She is walking* _____ .

2. (the girl / have / dinner / ? ➡ No / read / a book)
   Q: _____ ?
   A: _____ .

3. (the women / take / a shower / ? ➡ No / take / a picture)
   Q: _____ ?
   A: _____ .

What + be + S + Ⓥ -ing?

Grammar focus

Q: **What** is she do**ing**?
A: She is drinking milk.

Q: **Who** is play**ing** the drum?
A: Tiffany is playing the drum.

1. What과 Who의 차이는 무엇인가요?

　what은 문장에서 목적어의 역할을 하고, '무엇을'이라는 뜻이에요. who는 문장에서 주어의 역할을 하며, '누가'라는 의미로 쓰입니다.

Wh-word	Be-verb	Subject	Base verb+Ⓥ-ing
What	am	I	doing?
	are	you	
	is	he / she	
	is	Tom / Mary / Peter / it	
	are	we / they	

Subject	Be-verb	Base verb+Ⓥ-ing
Who	is	singing?
		cooking?
		standing?

2. wh-로 시작하는 의문문의 답은 어떻게 하나요?

　대답은 주어가 단수일 때 〈주어(단수)+is+Ⓥ-ing ～〉, 주어가 복수일 때 〈주어(복수)+are+Ⓥ-ing ～〉로 해요.

Go for it!

A. Circle the correct word.

1. (What / Who) is cooking?

2. (What / Who) is he doing?

3. (What / Who) is she doing?

4. (What / Who) is your dog doing?

5. (What / Who) is reading a book?

6. (What / Who) is the woman doing?

7. (What / Who) is sitting on the bench?

B. Match questions and answers.

1. Who is sleeping?

2. What is he doing?

3. What are they doing?

4. Who is riding a bicycle?

They are watching a movie.

Kathy is riding a bicycle.

He is drinking juice.

Jane is sleeping.

C. Choose and write answers.

1.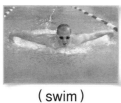
   (Scott)

   Q: (What are / (Who is)) flying a kite?
   A: *Scott is flying a kite* .

2.
   (swim)

   Q: (What is / Who is) Bob doing?
   A: _____ .

3.
   (play tennis)

   Q: (What is / Who is) Jessica doing?
   A: _____ .

4.
   (Jason and Susan)

   Q: (What is / Who is) painting the house?
   A: _____ .

D. Make questions.

1. who / drink / water → *Who is drinking water* ?

2. what / your sister / do → _____ ?

3. who / play / the piano → _____ ?

4. what / the children / do → _____ ?

5. who / drive / a car → _____ ?

Grammar in Writing

A. Look at the answers and complete the questions.

1. Q: What _____ *is he drinking* _____?
   A: He is drinking milk.

2. Q: Who _____?
   A: Kevin is flying a kite.

3. Q: What _____?
   A: She is studying Korean.

4. Q: Who _____?
   A: My sister is sitting on the sofa.

5. Q: What _____?
   A: They are making cookies.

B. Look and write questions and answers.

(Jennifer)   (watch a movie)

(Scott)   (have breakfast)

(Tiffany)   (walk to school)

1. *Who is playing the guitar* _____?
   Jennifer is playing the guitar.
2. What are they doing?
   _____.
3. _____?
   Scott is playing volleyball.
4. What are Bob and Lisa doing?
   _____.
5. _____?
   Tiffany is sitting on the bench.
6. What are they doing?
   _____.

Chapter 5
Prepositions & Adjectives

Unit 1. **P**repositions of **P**lace

Unit 2. **A**djective + **N**oun

Unit 3. **A**djective + **N**oun / **B**e + **A**djective

Unit 4. **C**omparative **A**djectives

Prepositions of Place

Grammar focus

Q: Where is your mother?
A: She is **on** the bench.

Q: Where is your car?
A: It is **behind** the bicycle.

1. 장소의 전치사가 뭐예요?
   장소의 전치사는 명사 앞에 와서 어떤 장소나, 위치에 대한 정보를 알려주는 역할을 해요.

2. 장소의 전치사는 어떤 것들이 있나요?
   in(안에), on(위에), under(아래), behind(뒤에), in front of(앞에), next to(옆에)라는 전치사들이 있어요. 주로 be동사와 함께 쓰여 '~에 있다'라는 뜻이 됩니다.

Usage

Q: Where is the dog?
A: It is **in** the box.

Q: Where is the cat?
A: It is **on** the box.

Q: Where is the dog?
A: It is **under** the chair.

Q: Look at the dog.
A: It is **next to** the box.

Q: Look at the cat.
A: It is **behind** the box.

Q: Look at the mouse.
A: It is **in front of** the box.

Go for it!

A. Look and circle the correct word.

1.

(behind the tree / ~~under the tree~~)

2.

(next to the basket / in the basket)

3.

(behind the door / in front of the door)

B. Circle the correct word.

1. (~~Where is~~ / Where are) the tree?

2. (Where is / Where are) the women?

3. (Where is / Where are) your friends?

4. (Where is / Where are) the man?

5. (Where is / Where are) the giraffe?

6. (Where is / Where are) your socks?

C. Look and fill in the blanks.

1.

   Q: Where is the boat?
   A: It is ___*under*___ the bridge.

2.

   Q: Where is your teacher?
   A: She is _____ the bench.

3.

   Q: Where is Tom?
   A: He is _____ Sunny.

4.

   Q: Where is the bicycle?
   A: It is _____ the bus.

D. Read and wrtie *where is* or *where are*.

1. Q: ___*Where is*___ the dog?   A: It is under the tree.

2. Q: _____ the babies?   A: They are on the bed.

3. Q: _____ your cell phone?   A: It is on the table.

4. Q: _____ the pencils?   A: They are in the pencil case.

Grammar in Writing

A. Read and make questions.

1. Q: *Where is the boy* ? A: The boy is in front of the door.

2. Q: _____ ? A: The girls are in the classroom.

3. Q: _____ ? A: The children are under the tree.

4. Q: _____ ? A: The bicycle is behind the car.

5. Q: _____ ? A: The backpack is under the bed.

6. Q: _____ ? A: The women are in front of the tree.

B. Read and make answers.

1.

Q: Is the woman next to the bed?
A: *No, she isn't* . *She is on the bed* .

2.

Q: Is the girl in front of the table?
A: _____ . _____ .

3.

Q: Is the man behind the woman?
A: _____ . _____ .

4.

Q: Are Bob and Kelly on the car?
A: _____ . _____ .

Adjective + Noun

Grammar focus

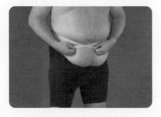

He is a **fat** man.

She has **beautiful** eyes.

1. 형용사가 뭐예요?

형용사는 명사 앞에 와서 명사의 성질, 상태, 색깔, 모양 등을 표현해 주는 말이에요. 명사를 구체적으로 설명하는 역할을 해요.

관사	형용사	명사
a	big small long short	skirt
an	expensive honest	car boy
X	kind unkind	girls

관사	형용사	명사
a	happy sad fat thin hungry	woman
X	delicious hot	pizza

＊복수명사나 셀 수 없는 명사 앞에는 관사 a/an을 쓰지 않아요.

Usage

She has **long** hair.

They are **green** apples.

It is **hot** coffee.

Go for it!

A. Look and circle.

1.
(a pretty girl / an ugly boy)

2.
(a sad student / a happy student)

3.
(a fat woman / a thin woman)

4.
(a yellow orange / a red orange)

B. Match the opposites.

1. small   •   • short

2. thin   •   • hot

3. clean   •   • dirty

4. cold   •   • fat

5. tall   •   • big

C. Look and rewrite the sentence.

1.

   It is a clock.

   It is a square clock . (square)

2.

   She has a shopping bag.

   _____ . (red)

3.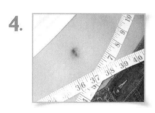

   It is a suitcase.

   _____ . (heavy)

4.

   She is a woman.

   _____ . (thin)

D. Combine two sentences.

1. It is a hat. ➕ It is blue.

   ➡ *It is a blue hat* .

2. Kelly is a girl. ➕ She is prettey.

   ➡ _____ .

3. They are trees. ➕ They are tall.

   ➡ _____ .

4. She has eyes. ➕ They are brown.

   ➡ _____ .

Grammar in Writing

A. Match and make sentences.

1. long hair

2. big ball

3. slow animal

4. hot coffee

It _____.

It _____*is long hair*_____.

It _____.

It _____.

B. Read and make answers.

1.

(happy)

A: Are they sad students?

B: *No, they aren't* .

They are happy students .

2.

(cold)

A: Is it hot food?

B: _____.

_____.

3.

(small)

A: Are they big ants?

B: _____.

_____.

4.

(thin)

A: Is she a fat woman?

B: _____.

_____.

Adjective + Noun / Be + Adjective

Grammar focus

She is a **happy** woman.
The woman is **happy**.

It is a **small** mouse.
The mouse is **small**.

1. 형용사의 역할은 무엇인가요?

크게 두 가지가 있어요. 명사의 바로 앞에서 명사를 꾸며주거나 또는 be동사 뒤에 위치하여 주어인 명사를 설명해 주는 역할을 해요.

형용사＋명사	Be동사＋형용사
It is a big tree. They are kind doctors.	The tree is big. The doctors are kind.

Usage

It isn't an **old** car.
It is a **new** car.
The car is **new**.

It isn't a **slow** animal.
It is a **fast** animal.
The animal is **fast**.

Go for it!

A. Look, circle and write.

1.

fat / (thin)

She is a _____thin_____ woman.
The woman ___is thin___ .

2.

yellow / blue

It is a _____ banana.
The banana _____ .

3.

angry / happy

They are _____ girls.
The girls _____ .

4.

long / short

It is a _____ pencil.
The pencil _____ .

B. Read and circle the correct word.

1. This camera is (new / (old)). I want a new camera.

2. Open the window. We need (dirty / clean) air.

3. Don't eat fast food too much. You are very (thin / fat).

C. Write the opposite words.

1. The snake is long.   → It isn't _____*short*_____ .

2. Tiffany is young.   → She isn't _____ .

3. Bob is sad.   → He isn't _____ .

4. The basketball player is tall.   → He isn't _____ .

D. Match and complete the sentences.

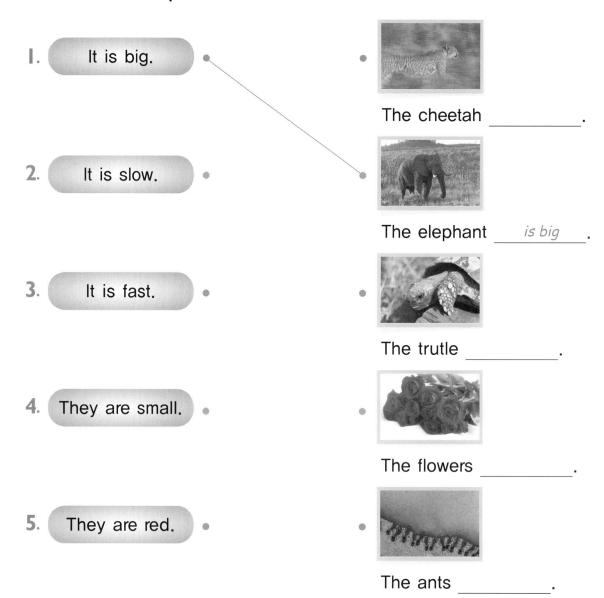

1. It is big. •

    The cheetah _____ .

2. It is slow. •

    The elephant _____*is big*_____ .

3. It is fast. •

    The trutle _____ .

4. They are small. •

    The flowers _____ .

5. They are red. •

    The ants _____ .

Grammar in Writing

A. Look and write.

1.
   (fast)

   It _____is a fast_____ airplane.
   The airplane _____is fast_____ .

2.
   (light)

   They _____ boxes.
   The boxes _____ .

3.
   (big)

   It _____ house.
   The house _____ .

B. Read and make answers.

1. Q: Is the girl happy?
   A: _Yes, she is_____ . _She is a happy girl_____ .

2. Q: Is the nurse kind?
   A: _____ . _____ .

3. Q: Are the students tall?
   A: _____ . _____ .

4. Q: Are the women pretty?
   A: _____ . _____ .

Comparative Adjectives

Grammar focus

The deer is fast.
The cheetah is **faster than** the deer.

The bicycle is expensive.
The car is **more** expensive **than** the bicycle.

1. 비교급이 뭐예요?

두 가지의 비슷한 대상을 두고 '어느 것이 더 좋은지, 또는 누가 더 뚱뚱한지'와 같이 서로를 비교하는 표현을 비교급이라고 해요. 〈비교급+than〉의 형태로 쓰고, '~보다 더 ~하다'라는 의미예요.

2. 비교급은 어떻게 만드나요?

❶ 대부분의 형용사 끝에 -er을 붙여요. 당연히 -e로 끝나는 단어는 -r만 붙이면 돼요.

long – long**er**　　　　tall – tall**er**　　　　small – small**er**　　　　nice – nic**er**

❷ 1음절의 단어가 〈단모음+단자음〉으로 끝나는 단어는 마지막 자음을 하나 더 쓰고 -er을 붙여요.

hot – hott**er**　　　　fat – fatt**er**　　　　big – bigg**er**

❸ y로 끝나는 단어는 끝의 y를 i로 고치고 -er을 붙여요.

happy – happ**ier**　　　　busy – bus**ier**　　　　heavy – heav**ier**

❹ 형용사의 음절이 2음절 이상인 경우 형용사 앞에 more을 붙여요.

beautiful – **more** beautiful　　　　expensive – **more** expensive
interesting – **more** interesting　　　　important – **more** important

Go for it!

A. Write the comparatives.

Adjectives	Comparatives	Adjectives	Comparatives
tall	_taller_ than	slow	_____ than
small	_____ than	fast	_____ than
short	_____ than	big	_____ than
hot	_____ than	thin	_____ than
fat	_____ than	happy	_____ than
heavy	_____ than	easy	_____ than
pretty	_____ than	expensive	_____ than
famous	_____ than	interesting	_____ than

B. Circle the correct word.

1. An elephant is (big / (bigger)) than a mouse.

2. This car is (expensiver / more expensive) than that one.

3. Kelly is (thiner / thinner) than her husband.

4. The Amazon is (longer / more long) than the Nile.

C. Look and complete sentences.

1. His hair is _____*shorter than*_____ her hair. (short)

2. The man is _____ the woman. (fat)

3. The woman is _____ the man. (thin)

4. Sunny is _____ Brian. (popular)

5. The boy is _____ the girl. (young)

D. Read and rank.

1. John is taller than Kevin. Bob is taller than John.

   Bob > John > Kevin _____.

2. Nancy is faster than Sunny. Tiffany is faster than Nancy.

   _____.

3. The pencil is cheaper than the bag. The iPhone is more expensive than the bag.

   _____.

E. Correct the underlined word.

1. Math is <u>difficult</u> than English.   ➡   *more difficult*

2. The snail is <u>slow</u> than the turtle.   ➡   _____

3. *Avatar* is more interesting <u>that</u> *Spider-man*. ➡ _____

4. The bicycle is <u>expensive</u> than my laptop.   ➡   _____

Grammar in Writing

A. Look and write.

1. Africa: small / Asia: big

   Africa _____ *is smaller than Asia* _____.

   Asia _____ *is bigger than Africa* _____.

2. The Nile: long / The Han river: short

   The Nile _____.

   The Han river _____.

3. The Sun: big / The Earth: small

   The Sun _____.

   The Earth _____.

4. Mt. Everest: high / Mt. Baekdu: low

   Mt. Everest _____.

   Mt. Baekdu _____.

B. Write comparisons in the blanks.

1.

   (Bob / Jane / short)

   Bob's hair *is shorter* _____

   than Jane's hair   .

2.

   (Linda / Eric / thin)

   Linda _____

   .

Chapter 6
Helping Verbs & Past Tense

Can / May ~ ?

Grammar focus

Q: **Can** she play the drum?
A: Yes, she **can**.

Q: **May**(**Can**) I ask you a question?
A: Sure.

1. 조동사 can은 어떤 의미가 있나요?
can은 '~할 수 있다'는 능력(ability)을 나타내고, 허락을 나타낼 때는 '~해도 좋다'는 의미입니다.

2. 조동사 may는 어떤 의미인가요?
50% 이하의 추측이나 가능성(guess, possibility) 또는 허락(permission)을 나타내요. 추측일 때 may는 '~일런지 모른다'의 뜻이고 허락을 나타낼 때는 '~해도 좋다'의 뜻이 돼요.
May I ~?와 Can I ~ ?는 '~을 해도 좋은지'를 상대방에게 물어보며 허락을 요청하거나 부탁할 때 쓰는 표현이에요.

Usage

Q: **Can** she dance?
A: Yes, she **can**.

Q: **May**(**Can**) I see
   your driver's licence?
A: Yes, of course. Here
   it is.

You **may** use my
digital camera.
(=You **can** use my
digital camera.)

Go for it!

A. Look at the underlined word and circle.

1. <u>Can</u> I watch TV tonight?

   (Possibility) / Ability

2. Tiffany <u>can</u> drive a car.

   Ability / Possibility

3. <u>Can</u> you speak Korean?

   Ability / Permission

4. You <u>may</u> use my cell phone.

   Permission / Possibility

5. <u>May</u> I sit here?

   Permission / Possibility

6. Bob <u>may</u> go to Mexico next year.

   Ability / Possibility

7. It <u>may</u> rain tomorrow.

   Permission / Possibility

B. Write *can* or *can't*.

1.

   The bear ___*can*___ swim.
   It ___*can't*___ fly.

2.

   The Kangaroos _____ climb trees.
   They _____ jump high.

C. Write *May* or *Can*.

1. ___*May / Can*___ I sit here?

2. _____ you speak French?

3. _____ Lisa play the guitar?

4. _____ I use your pen?

5. _____ your dad ski?

6. _____ I see your tickets, please?

D. Read and write answers.

1. Can Jessica dance?   Yes, ___*she can*___. No, ___*she can't*___.

2. May I come in?   Yes, _____. No, _____.

3. Can you go out and play? Yes, _____. No, _____.

4. Can the women cook?   Yes, _____. No, _____.

5. May I have some water?   Yes, _____. No, _____.

6. Can Peter play the guitar? Yes, _____. No, _____.

Grammar in Writing

A. Look at the pictures. Then write questions and answers.

1.
Q: *Can Sunny play the drum* ?
A: *Yes, she can* .
(Sunny can play the drum.)

2.
Q: _____ ?
A: _____ .
(The trutle can't run fast.)

3.
Q: _____ ?
A: _____ .
(Jason can't play tennis.)

4.
Q: _____ ?
A: _____ .
(Tiffany can fly a kite.)

B. Read and make questions.

1. I want some cookies.
   → *May(Can) I have some cookies* ? (have)

2. Lend me your digital camera.
   → _____ ? (borrow)

3. I will open the window.
   → _____ ? (open)

4. I want your bicycle.
   → _____ ? (ride)

unit 2 *S+was[were] ~*

Grammar focus

past | **was** a student |0 years ago.
| **wasn't** a doctor.

present | **am** a doctor now.

1. be동사의 과거는 어떻게 만드나요?

be동사의 과거형은 was와 were예요. 주어가 단수일 때는 was를 쓰고 주어가 복수일 때는 were을 써서 과거에 어떤 상태였는지를 설명해줍니다. 우리말로 '~이었다, ~에 있었다'의 뜻이에요.

2. 부정문은 어떻게 만들어요?

be동사 과거의 부정은 be동사 현재시제의 부정과 똑같이 be동사 뒤에 not을 붙여주면 돼요.

Subject(주어)	Affirmative(긍정)	Negative(부정)
I / He / She / It	was	was not(=wasn't)
You / We / They	were	were not(=weren't)

Usage

She **wasn't** fat.
She **was** thin.

He **wasn't** at the park.
He **was** at home.

They **weren't** teachers.
They **were** nurses.

Go for it!

A. Look and write.

		Positives		Negatives
1. I	⇒	*was*	⇒	*wasn't*
2. You	⇒	_____	⇒	_____
3. We	⇒	_____	⇒	_____
4. He	⇒	_____	⇒	_____
5. She	⇒	_____	⇒	_____
6. They	⇒	_____	⇒	_____
7. It	⇒	_____	⇒	_____
8. Kevin	⇒	_____	⇒	_____
9. Lisa and I	⇒	_____	⇒	_____
10. The women	⇒	_____	⇒	_____
11. Peter and Tom	⇒	_____	⇒	_____
12. Leaves	⇒	_____	⇒	_____
13. The water	⇒	_____	⇒	_____
14. The city	⇒	_____	⇒	_____

B. Write *was, were* or *wasn't, weren't*.

1.  They ___weren't___ at the classroom.

2.  He _____ a singer 5 years ago.

3.  They_____ happy yesterday.

4.  She _____ a farmer.

5. Bob and Brian _____ on the bench.

C. Make the sentences negative.

1. You were smart. ➡ *You weren't smart* _____.

2. The trees were tall. ➡ _____.

3. They were busy. ➡ _____.

4. We were at the gym. ➡ _____.

5. My mom was in Paris. ➡ _____.

Grammar in Writing

A. Rewrite the sentences.

1. Scott is a dentist now.
   ➡ *Scott was a dentist last year* . (last year)

2. It is very hot today.
   ➡ _____ . (yesterday)

3. My daddy isn't at home now.
   ➡ _____ . (2 hours ago)

4. The children are studying English now.
   ➡ _____ . (10 minutes ago)

B. Look at the chart and make sentences.

	10 years ago	Now
Bob	soccer player	actor
Linda	thin	fat
Ted	farmer	doctor
They	student	teacher

1. Bob *wasn't an actor ten years ago. He was a soccer player* .

2. Linda _____ .

3. Ted _____ .

4. They _____ .

unit 3 Was[Were] + S ~ ?

Grammar focus

Q **Was** Mozart a painter?
A: **No**, he **wasn't**. He **was** a musician.
Q: **Was** he Austrian?
A: **Yes**, he **was**.

1. be동사가 있는 문장의 과거 의문문은 어떻게 만드나요?
was나 were을 문장 맨 앞으로 보내고 문장 마지막에 물음표(?)를 쓰면 돼요. '~이었니?, ~에 있었니?'라는 뜻이에요.

2. 답은 어떻게 하나요?
대답은 긍정일 때 〈Yes, +주어+was / were〉, 부정일 때는 〈No, +주어+wasn't / weren't〉로 해요.

Usage

Q: **Was** she a tennis player?

A: **Yes**, she **was**.

No, she **wasn't**.
She **was** a violinist.

Q: **Were** they at the party?

A: **Yes**, they **were**.

No, they **weren't**.
They **were** at home.

Go for it!

A. Circle the correct word.

1. (**Was** / Were) she happy?

2. (Was / Were) he handsome?

3. (Was / Were) you at home?

4. (Was / Were) the nurse kind?

5. (Was / Were) it easy?

6. (Was / Were) Sunny sad?

7. (Was / Were) the books cheap?

8. (Was / Were) Lisa at the library?

9. (Was / Were) they at the museum?

10. (Was / Were) the pencils on the table?

B. Match and write.

1. Was she tired?

Yes, _____.

Yes, _____*she was*_____.

2. Were they in the classroom?

3. Was he a nurse?

Yes, _____.

4. Were you thin?

No, _____.

C. Look at the answers and complete the questions.

1.

   Q: _Was_ _he_ sad yesterday?

   A: Yes, he was.

2.

   Q: _____ _____ cheap?

   A: No, it wasn't. It was expensive

3.

   Q: _____ _____ a painter?

   A: No, she wasn't.
   She was a fashion model.

4.

   Q: _____ _____ in Korea?

   A: No, they weren't.
   They were in Egypt.

D. Put the words in the correct order.

1. she / a student / was ➡ _Was she a student_ ?

2. hungry / they / were ➡ _____ ?

3. exciting / was / the concert ➡ _____ ?

4. a taxi driver / were / you ➡ _____ ?

5. in Korea / we / were ➡ _____ ?

6. sick / Johnson / was ➡ _____ ?

Grammar in Writing

A. Look at the chart and write questions and answers.

No.	Name	Place	Yes(O)	No(X)
1.	Jason	at home	O	
2.	Nancy	at the library		X
3.	Karen	at school	O	
4.	Bob	at the bookstore		X
5.	Peter and Lisa	at the museum	O	

1. Q: *Was Jason at home* ?
   A: *Yes, he was* .

2. Q: _____ ?
   A: _____ .

3. Q: _____ ?
   A: _____ .

4. Q: _____ ?
   A: _____ .

5. Q: _____ ?
   A: _____ .

B. Read and make answers.

1.

(singer)

Q: Was he a dancer?

A: *No, he wasn't.* .

   He was a singer .

2.

(speed skater)

Q: Was he a figure skater?

A: _____ .

   _____ .

115

unit 4 — Regular Past Tense

Grammar focus

It **rained** yesterday.
He **needed** an umbrella.

1. 과거동사란 뭔가요?

일반동사의 과거형을 말하는 것으로 이미 지나간 일을 표현할 때 사용하는 동사예요. 현재와는 아무런 관련이 없고, '~했다, 했었다'의 뜻을 가져요.

2. 과거시제는 어떻게 만드나요?

과거시제를 만들 때도 규칙이 있어요.

❶ 대부분의 동사에 -ed를 붙여서 과거동사를 만들어요.

walk ➡ walk**ed**	rain ➡ rain**ed**	visit ➡ visit**ed**
play ➡ play**ed**	help ➡ help**ed**	paint ➡ paint**ed**
wash ➡ wash**ed**	talk ➡ talk**ed**	listen ➡ listen**ed**
clean ➡ clean**ed**		

❷ -e로 끝나는 동사는 그냥 -d만 붙이면 돼요.

dance ➡ dance**d**	live ➡ live**d**	like ➡ like**d**
love ➡ love**d**	hate ➡ hate**d**	hope ➡ hope**d**

❸ 동사 끝에 〈자음+y〉로 끝나면 y를 i로 고치고 -ed를 붙여요.

study ➡ stud**ied**	cry ➡ cr**ied**	try ➡ tr**ied**

Go for it!

A. Write the verbs in the past tense.

1. play   ⟹   _played_

2. walk   ⟹   _____

3. help   ⟹   _____

4. talk   ⟹   _____

5. wash   ⟹   _____

6. paint   ⟹   _____

7. rain   ⟹   _____

8. visit   ⟹   _____

9. clean   ⟹   _____

10. listen   ⟹   _____

11. dance   ⟹   _____

12. live   ⟹   _____

13. like   ⟹   _____

14. love   ⟹   _____

15. study   ⟹   _____

16. try   ⟹   _____

17. cry   ⟹   _____

18. need   ⟹   _____

19. hope   ⟹   _____

20. work   ⟹   _____

B. Check and fill in the blanks.

1.

   ☐ visited
   ☑ watched

   We ___watched___ TV.

2.

   ☐ rained
   ☐ studied

   Tiffany _____ English.

3.

   ☐ listened
   ☐ danced

   My mom _____ to music.

4.

   ☐ helped
   ☐ talked

   Lisa _____ on the phone.

C. Change the sentences to the past tense.

1. She brushes her teeth. ➡ *She brushed her teeth* _____.

2. He washes his face. ➡ _____.

3. The man loves his daughter. ➡ _____.

4. Nancy studies Japanese. ➡ _____.

5. Bob paints the door. ➡ _____.

6. I visit my grandparents. ➡ _____.

7. My uncle lives in Singapore. ➡ _____.

Grammar in Writing

A. Read and write with the information given.

Scott

⟨every day⟩	⟨yesterday⟩
play soccer	clean the window
listen to music	study Korean
walk in the park	cook spaghetti
watch TV	wash his car

1. *Scott plays soccer every day.*   *Scott cleaned the window yesterday* .

2. _____ . _____ .

3. _____ . _____ .

4. _____ . _____ .

B. Look and Write.

1.

(Susan / dance very well)

➡ *Susan danced very well* .

2.

(she / work in a hospital)

➡ _____ .

3.

(Lisa / listen to music)

➡ _____ .

4.

(Bob / wash an apple)

➡ _____ .

Irregular Past Tense

Grammar focus

She **went** shopping yesterday.
She **bought** a new bag.

1. 불규칙 과거동사가 뭐예요?

규칙적으로 동사에 -(e)d를 붙여 과거동사를 만들지 않고 자신만의 과거형을 갖는 동사를 말해요.

Past Tense – Irregular(불규칙 과거동사)		
go ➡ went	have ➡ had	come ➡ came
begin ➡ began	hear ➡ heard	find ➡ found
give ➡ gave	leave ➡ left	see ➡ saw
eat ➡ ate	make ➡ made	sing ➡ sang
write ➡ wrote	buy ➡ bought	read ➡ read
meet ➡ met	drive ➡ drove	sit ➡ sat
get ➡ got	speak ➡ spoke	ride ➡ rode

Usage

She **had** lunch.

They **sang** a song.

We **went** to the zoo.

Go for it!

A. Change the verbs to the past tense.

1. go → _____went_____

2. begin → _____

3. give → _____

4. eat → _____

5. write → _____

6. meet → _____

7. get → _____

8. have → _____

9. hear → _____

10. leave → _____

11. make → _____

12. buy → _____

13. drive → _____

14. speak → _____

15. come → _____

16. find → _____

17. see → _____

18. sing → _____

19. read → _____

20. sit → _____

21. ride → _____

B. Change the verbs to the past tense.

1.

Linda _drove_ a car.
(drive)

2.

She _____ a letter.
(write)

3.

My mom _____ on the bench.
(sit)

4.

He _____ a gift.
(buy)

5.

I _____ my friend.
(meet)

6.

My dad _____ a book.
(read)

C. Circle the wrong word and correct it.

1. I buied a hat yesterday.

   ➡ _I bought a hat yesterday_ .

2. Peter goed to the park last Sunday.

   ➡ _____ .

3. My mom gived me some money.

   ➡ _____ .

4. She comed to the party.

   ➡ _____ .

Grammar in Writing

A. Put the words in the correct order.

1. went / Bob / to / Japan

   ➡ *Bob went to Japan* .

2. yesterday morning / milk / drank / I

   ➡ _____ .

3. shopping / my mom / went

   ➡ _____ .

4. at 7:00 yesterday / they / breakfast / had

   ➡ _____ .

B. Look at the pictures and write answers.

1.

   (sing a song)

   Q: What did the girls do yesterday?

   A: *They sang a song* .

2.

   (go to school)

   Q: Where did they go yesterday?

   A: _____ .

3.

   (buy a bag)

   Q: What did Karen buy yesterday?

   A: _____ .

4.

   (write a letter)

   Q: What did Lucy write yesterday?

   A: _____ .